First published 2020
© Wooden Books Ltd 2020

Published by Wooden Books Ltd.
Glastonbury, Somerset

British Library Cataloguing in Publication Data
McDonnell, H.
Orkney

A CIP catalogue record for this book
may be obtained from the British Library

ISBN-10: 1-904263-28-3
ISBN-13: 978-1-904263-28-9

Designed and typeset in Glastonbury, UK.

Printed in China on 100% FSC
approved sustainable papers by FSC
RR Donnelley Asia Printing Solutions Ltd.

WOODEN
BOOKS

ORKNEY

MEGALITHIC MARVEL
OF THE NORTHERN ISLES

Hector McDonnell

I am particularly indebted to the generous help of the director of the Ness excavation, Nick Card, and Caroline Wickham-Jones, one of Orkney's leading archaeologists and the author of several excellent books on its past (including '*Orkney, a Historical Guide*' and '*Between the Wind and Water, World Heritage Orkney*'). As she says 'the archaeological record of Orkney is, in many ways, without comparison. It is a record about which there is always something more to learn.' Thank you also to Sarah Mclean at the Orkney Library and Archive collection for her assistance with picture research. For all things Orcadian I highly recommend the website Orkneyjar.com. Finally thank you to Norman Ackroyd RA, for allowing us to reproduce so many of his beautiful aquatints of Orkney, they appear below and on pages 3, 14 and 47.

Above: The Stones of Stenness, aquatint etching by Norman Ackroyd RA, 1996.
Title page: The Old Man of Hoy, Orkney, from the Illustrated London News, 1873.
Title Page: The Ring of Brodgar, painting by John Frederick Miller, 1775.

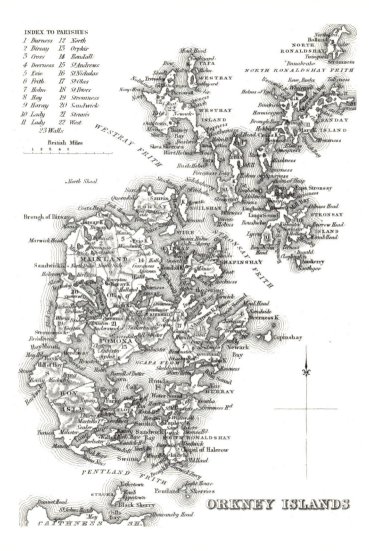

INDEX TO PARISHES

1	Burness	12	North
2	Birsay	13	Orphir
3	Cross	14	Rendall
4	Deerness	15	St Andrews
5	Evie	16	St Nicholas
6	Firth	17	St Olas
7	Holm	18	St Peters
8	Hoy	19	Stronness
9	Harray	20	Sandwick
10	Lady	21	Stennis
11	Lady	22	West
	23 Walls		

British Miles

1 2 3 4 5

ORKNEY ISLANDS

INTRODUCTION

AT THE END OF THE ICE AGE, the ice sheets and glaciers that had covered Scotland for tens of thousands of years melted. As a result, bands of hunter gatherers moved north across the newly opened lands, and reached Orkney, an archipelago of some 70 islands off the north-eastern tip of Scotland, for the very first time.

The oldest site so far identified is a camp on Stronsay, which has a carbon date of circa 7000 BC, while a charred hazelnut shell from a site at Longhowe in Tankerness is circa 6820–6660 BC. A spread of worked stone pieces left after tool-making has also been found as 'lithic scatters' at Seatter, South Ettit, Wideford Hill, Valdigar and the Loch of Stenness along with a few small polished stone tools, which are rarities on Mesolithic sites.

The world of these nomads was badly disrupted around 6000 BC, when a large part of the continental shelf collapsed off the west coast of Norway. This caused a tsunami which was about 25 metres (82 ft) high when it hit Orkney, before devastating the coastal regions of northern Scotland. However, the hunter gathering way of life seems to have recovered and continued until Neolithic people arrived, two thousand years later. This is where our story begins.

This book is intended to give its readers an overview of Orkney's prehistory and its remarkable remains. There were some astonishing developments here during the Neolithic and Bronze Age periods, and we now know that the influence of Orkney's megalithic culture extended throughout the British Isles.

NEOLITHIC ORKNEY
settlers from the fertile crescent

The Neolithic farming communities who settled across Orkney ultimately created a culture of exceptional grandeur. Some of its developments are either without parallel elsewhere or else are amongst the earliest identified, including two of the period's greatest innovations, the stone circles and henges.

The Neolithic culture sprang from the domestication of livestock and crops in the Near East around the ninth millennium BC, as the descendants of these people gradually spread out across Europe over the following millennia. They brought red deer with them, introduced pottery and established permanent settlements rather than moving with the seasons as the hunter gatherers did. There seems to have been little interbreeding between the earlier groups and the incoming Neolithic settlers, who generally retained the olive skin, brown eyes and dark hair of their Near Eastern ancestors.

One route of this Neolithic spread was along the Mediterranean and then up the Atlantic coastlines while another came up through Central Europe and then spread west. Both traditions influenced the settlement of the British Isles, including Orkney, although most of the original settlement was by the sea-going Atlantic coast settlers.

Dunnet Head.   Orkney Islands, from the East.   Hoy

Kame of Hoy   Artist's proof   '96

St John's Head   Colour proof   '96

3

EARLIER MONUMENTS
great earthworks and stones

As the Neolithic culture spread westwards, certain traditions developed, like the idea that settlements should maintain 'ancestor houses' for the dead. These started as wooden structures, that were then covered with earth and stones and out of which developed the megalithic shrines, passage graves and sacred mounds of Europe's Atlantic fringe, which spread northwards from Iberia to Norway, Orkney included.

Great ritual sites arose in several places during this spread, most famously on Malta and in Brittany, many designed with attention to the changing risings and settings of the sun, moon and other celestial bodies. Indeed the first Mesolithic hunter gatherers to arrive at Crathes in Aberdeenshire after the last Ice Age, created alignments by putting large posts in the ground to help observe the sun and the moon's movements. The Neolithic henges and stone circles were thus made by people with long traditions about watching the yearly changes of the heavenly bodies and of coming together to make large banked and ditched places for communal activities.

Enclosure No I.

16th April
27th August

15

Enclosure No II.

15th April
26th August

14
16

4th November
7th February

Mid-quater-days

N

Left: Circa 5000–4700 BC, after Neolithic communities had settled across central Europe, they created dozens of roughly round ritual sites or "Rondels," like this one at the Sormás Török-földek site in Hungary.

Below: Neolithic rondels are ditched and banked enclosures, mostly found along the Danube and Elbe river basins. They had walls of large wooden beams with openings, which let in midsummer dawn and sunset, such as the example below at Goseck, Saxony-Anhalt, Germany. Further west and in the British Isles in the early Neolithic, causewayed enclosures formed meeting places where people left offerings of bones, pottery and flints. These were followed in the British Isles by cursuses, long banked enclosures, some miles long, possibly used for archery or hunting displays.

THE KNAP OF HOWAR
Orkney's Neolithic farms

Neolithic people reached Orkney circa 4000 BC, and originally built timber-framed houses as they had elsewhere. The foundations of some have been found, including at Wideford and Wyre, but as wood was scarce the settlers turned to a plentiful local resource, a sedimentary rock which split into manageable slabs. As a result, Neolithic Orkney is unusually rich in stone structures.

For example, circa 3700 BC a wooden-framed farmstead at the Knap of Howar on the island of Papa Westray was replaced by a stone structure (*see facing page*). This is the oldest surviving farmhouse in northern Europe and consists of two adjacent thick-walled rectangular buildings, with rounded ends and low doorways and linked by a passageway. Being structurally sound they needed little more than occasional repairs, and were lived in for nine hundred years. This was unusually long, but many of Orkney's Neolithic stone houses were used for centuries.

Light and warmth were major concerns in Neolithic houses, and as in recent traditional societies, activities in each house probably took place in specific areas and at particular times as daylight moved round the room. The fire in the hearth was equally important; traditional societies often believed that a fire had to be maintained to keep a house alive, and that it would be formally extinguished only when the house was abandoned. Similar customs seems to have been practiced in Neolithic Orkney, where the positioning, design and treatment of their hearths were clearly matters of great significance.

Nevertheless, it was a hard existence and those who survived childhood mostly died in their twenties or thirties. Few reached fifty.

Above: Artist's impression of the Knap of Howar, Papa Westray, the oldest surviving farmhouse in northern Europe. Although life was precarious, even when harvests were poor and livestock in short supply, the Orcadians had wild resources to support them. The Knap of Howar's midden, for example, contained the bones of deer, fish, birds, seals and whales as well as cattle, sheep and pigs. Below: Analysis of the Knap of Howar by Nicholas Cope. The exterior length of the smaller building is the same as the interior length of the larger.

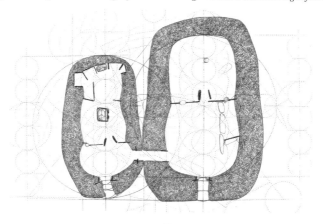

THE FIRST MEGALITHIC TOMBS
Taversöe Tuick's Stalled Cairns, Rousay

Orkney's Neolithic passage graves derived from traditions developed in Caithness and seem to have been ancestor shrines for each little community. Often built at prominent places near the farmed land, the similarities of these tombs suggest their construction was supervised by specialists, maybe shamans or priests. Each consisted of a mortuary chamber reached down a straight low 1m to 6.5m passageway that entered the chamber at a narrow end. As a result each tomb makes a straight alignment, mostly pointing at a significant local feature, such as a hill top, settlement or standing stone. Several point to the south-east mid-winter moonrise and sunrise while others are oriented to the cross-quarter sunrises, those days four 'quarter days' halfway between the equinoxes and solstices, which traditionally divided the seasons, such as Beltane at the end of April, for the beginning of summer, and Lammas at its end, or Samhain in early November at the onset of winter and Imbolc at its conclusion in early February (to use the Celtic names).

At their inner ends, pairs of portal stones mark the entry to the main chambers which were over two metres high, so people could stand in them. The chambers were about 1½ to 2 metres wide and had 50cm deep slabs protruding out at intervals along their length with 50cm high stone benches between them making 1m to 2.5m long bench-like side compartments for the remains of the dead. A narrow way ran down the middle of each chamber between these stalls to a partitioned area at its far end, which must have been particularly significant; each rear wall had a stone slab about a metre high built into it, tilting slightly backwards, while stone shelves often ran along the side walls above the slab, upon which were put further human remains.

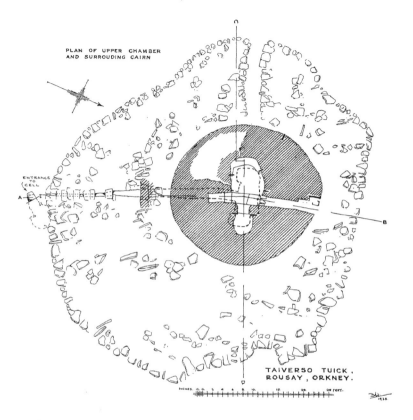

PLAN OF UPPER CHAMBER
AND SURROUDING CAIRN

ENTRANCE
TO
CELL

A

B

TAIVERSO TUICK.
ROUSAY, ORKNEY.

Above: Taversöe Tuick's Stalled Cairns, Rousay, excavated in 1937 by Callander & Grant, is named from the Old Norse tafr (sacrifice) / taufr (magic) + 'öe' / 'tuick' (hill). This cairn is unique, as it has three chambers on different levels in it, all built at the same time. The two main chambers are set one above the other, each with its own entrance passage. The 3.4m entrance to the upper 5m × 2m two-stalled chamber is on the north side, while the 6m entrance to the lower 4m × 1.5m four-stalled chamber is on the south side, close to the tiny third 1.6m x 1.1m chamber. While cremated bones of three or four people and a child were found in the main chambers, only three pots were found in the third chamber, suggesting it may have been used for leaving offerings or communicating with the ancestors.

CALF OF EDAY LONG CAIRN
north east of Eday

This cairn was excavated in 1936. The original tomb had two small cells under a little cairn, as was typical in Caithness, but then a bigger stalled tomb was built beside it, with its own cairn and entrance passage. Finally, a large rectangular cairn was raised over them both, but only the later tomb's entrance was preserved. Shards of Unstan pottery, flint tools and two stones axes were found in the stalled chamber, but the soil was too acidic to preserve any human remains.

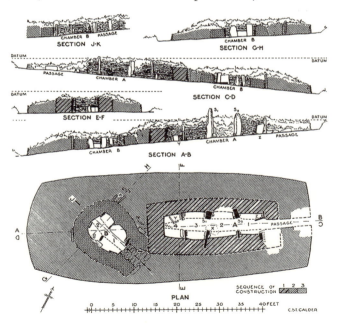

THE KNOWE OF YARSO

isle of Rousay

Bones from twenty-nine skeletons were found here, with many of the skulls set along the base of the walls in the innermost compartment. At least thirty-six red deer were also interred in the Knowe, suggesting that deer were the animal totems of this community.

These tombs are often called 'Stalled Cairns' as cairns were built over each one and the bench-like compartments in the tombs resemble cattle stalls. The earliest tombs were small, with only two or four compartments, but later ones had many more. There are about sixty in all on Orkney, including the islands of Rousay, Westray and Eday. These family mausoleums were often used for hundreds of years.

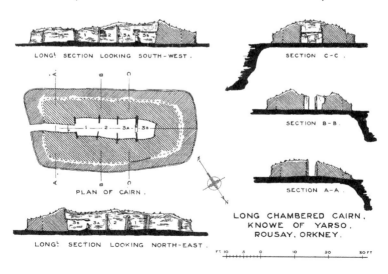

LONG.ᵗ SECTION LOOKING SOUTH-WEST.

SECTION C-C.

PLAN OF CAIRN.

SECTION B-B.

SECTION A-A.

LONG CHAMBERED CAIRN,
KNOWE OF YARSO,
ROUSAY, ORKNEY.

LONG.ᵗ SECTION LOOKING NORTH-EAST.

FT 10   5   0   10   20   50 FT

MIDHOWE STALLED CAIRN
isle of Rousay

The Midhowe tomb, on Rousay's western shore, was used from the Neolithic into the Beaker Period (*see pages 46–53*). Some of its walls are still over head height and its mound was originally about 30m long and 9m wide (100 × 30 ft). The chamber originally had only two or three stalls, but was lengthened to hold twelve. After the main chamber's roof collapsed, circa 2300 BC, two typical Beaker Culture type burials were left in the rubble. In 1932, the landowner of Midhowe organised its excavation and found a 23m (75 ft) long chamber. On the stone benches of its twelve stalls the remains of seventeen adults, six youths and two infants were laid out with their backs to the central passage.

Many animal bones were found here, from oxen and sheep, and also limpet shells, fish bones, bird bones (skuas, cormorants, buzzards, eagles, gannets, and carrion-crows) and some red deer antlers.

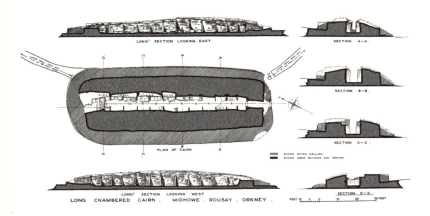

LONG¹ SECTION LOOKING EAST

SECTION A–A.

SECTION B–B.

SECTION C–C.

PLAN OF CAIRN

SHOWS OUTER WALLING
SHOWS INNER BUILDING AND GROUND

LONG¹ SECTION LOOKING WEST

LONG CHAMBERED CAIRN . MIDHOWE . ROUSAY . ORKNEY .

SECTION D–D.

FEET 10 5 0   10   20   30 FEET

KNOWE OF RAMSAY
also on Rousay

Some of the finest surviving stalled cairns are found on the island of Rousay. It has fifteen in all, many with their facing stones arranged in herringbone patterns. The largest, the Knowe of Ramsay, has fourteen stalls. During its excavation in 1936, few artifacts and human remains were discovered. However, bones of red deer, sheep, ox, great auk, bittern, cormorant, curlew, duck, sea or white-tailed eagle, pink-footed goose, and conger eel were found.

These tombs kept the community's ancestors close by, declaring a right to the land or maintaining a connection to the spirit Otherworld. The entrance passageways, like birth canals to a world beyond, vary from 1 to 6.5m in length. Typically under a metre high, people must have crawled along them to visit the ancestors or drag in the dead.

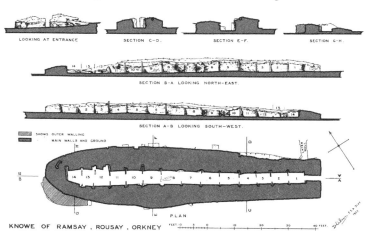

KNOWE OF RAMSAY, ROUSAY, ORKNEY

CATASTROPHE
an environmental disaster

Circa 3200–3190 BC, after Orkney's Neolithic culture had flourished for about 800 years, there seems to have been a major environmental upset. Tree rings from the British Isles indicate there was almost no growth for these ten years, so sunlight must have been severely reduced, probably by dust or ash particles in the atmosphere caused by a volcanic eruption or a large asteroid impact.

A huge spike in sulphate levels in the Greenland ice cores fifty years after the 3200 BC trauma suggests a second violent disturbance, presumably volcanic. These events seem to have led to the collapse of many farming communities. Pollen analysis suggests that woods and scrub grew back over abandoned fields post 3200 BC, with many settlements disappearing and herd rearing replacing crop growing.

15

THE STONES OF STENNESS

the first stone henge

The response of the Orcadians to a decade without summers was to build a series of very large structures, one of the first of which was the henge and stone circle known as the Stones of Stenness, the tallest of whose four remaining stones top 6m (19 ft), inside a 44m (144 ft) circle.

Stenness and the Ring of Brodgar (*see page 42*) are often thought of as a pair but were in fact erected many centuries apart. An 18th-century antiquarian said they were locally known as the 'Temple of the Sun' (Brodgar) and the 'Temple of the Moon' (Stenness), names that may reflect their original uses. Regardless, Stenness is the oldest henge and stone circle known anywhere in the world. Built around 3100 BC, its rock-cut ditch measures 4m across and 2.3m deep, while its single entrance causeway looks towards the great building at Barnhouse (*see page 30*). Originally intended to have twelve megaliths in its circle, only ten were ever erected. The extant stones were quarried at a considerable distance from Stenness, with over a dozen people needed to carry each one, so its creation was a massive undertaking.

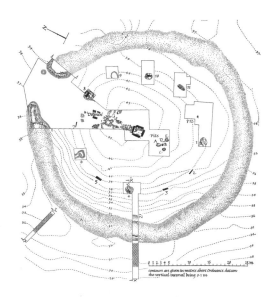

Left: Plan of the Stones of Stenness. The Stones stand on a clay platform inside a circular ditch with one entrance. Stenness has the same approximate radio carbon date (c.3100 BC) as early structures on the Ness of Brodgar, the stone circle of Calanais on Lewis, and the Class 1 henges at Stonehenge and Llandygai in North Wales. Although is not certain where the impetus for this new phase of ritually focussed construction began, it increasingly looks as though the original concepts were first combined on Orkney.

Facing page: Drawing of the Stones of Stenness by James Wright (National Galleries of Scotland).

Below: The Stone of Stenness, aquatint from William Daniell's A Voyage Around Great Britain, 1814

contours are given in metres above Ordnance datum the vertical interval being 0·1 m

Stones of Stenness. Orkney.

NEOLITHIC CONCEPTS
sun, moon and stars

The Orcadians, like all early societies, had strong ideas about the great entities in the sky and their relationship with life and fertility on earth. In particular the sun's yearly journey from warmth at its highest summer trajectory to the cold of its lowest in midwinter, combined with the moon's monthly rhythm of its phases and the nine-month appearances of Venus as a morning and then as an evening star.

At least one Stenness alignment marks a moment in the sun's cycle and several are directed at those of the moon, which makes a remarkable display in such northern latitudes. Every 18.6 years, at 'major lunar standstill', the moon rises at its most northerly position on the horizon and reaches its highest point in the sky, but just two weeks later, it rises at its most southerly position and rolls across the hill tops before setting again shortly after. The dark period of new moon then followed.

The moon's behaviour at the standstill will have caused awe, but at least Neolithic people could work out when these would happen, even including when the sun and moon might have eclipses. However, the 3200 BC event did not fit into any calculations, making it exceptionally disturbing. This may have made the Orcadians feel that they must appease the forces they depended upon in some exceptional way.

Facing page: Incised stone from chambered cairn, Eday.   Above: Moonlit Orcadian scene.   Below: The Dwarfie Stane, Hoy. A huge block of red sandstone with Neolithic carved chambers on either side. A large square stone closed the entrance. There are pecked patterns on the walls of the chamber.

BELIEFS, MYTHS AND RITUALS
dancing, beer and henbane

We cannot now know exactly what rites and rituals were done at these sites, but a brief text that may derive from the lost books of the 4th century BC historian and geographer Hecataeus of Abdera may offer some clues. The text describes an 'Island of the Hyperboreans' beyond the home of the north wind, whose inhabitants said that Apollo's mother Leto had given birth to him there. They had 'a sacred enclosure dedicated to him as well as a magnificent spherical temple' and the god came back to visit his birthplace every nineteen years.

> *'They also say that the moon, as viewed from this island, appears to be but a little distance above the Earth and to have prominences like those of the Earth, which are visible to the naked eye. The account is also given that the god visits the island every nineteen years, the period in which the return of the stars to the same place in the heavens is accomplished…At the time of the appearance of the god they both play on the cithara and dance continuously through the night from the vernal equinox until the rising of the Pleiades.'*

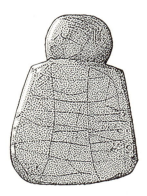

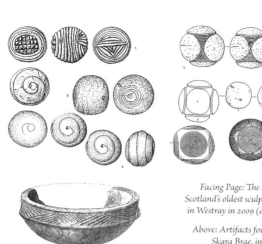

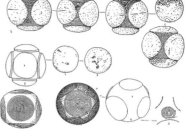

Facing Page: The 4cm tall Orkney Venus, Scotland's oldest sculpture of a human, discovered in Westray in 2009 (drawing Historic Scotland).

Above: Artifacts found during excavations at Skara Brae, including carved balls.

Left and below: Flat-bottomed grooved ware pottery (left from Unstan, page 26) was invented on Orkney at about the same time as Stenness was raised and then copied all over the British Isles, as further henges and stone circles were put up. Orkney must therefore have had a central role in the spread of these new ideas. Residues of substances possibly related to beer production have been found on some while others had traces of henbane, a strong hallucinogen.

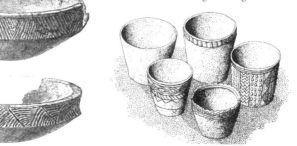

ISBISTER CAIRN, S. RONALDSAY
the 'Tomb of the Eagles'

Isbister Cairn is thought to date back to about 3000 BC, and like Unstan (*see page 26*), remained in use into the Beaker Period, after circa 2300 BC. Excavations revealed the bones of over 342 people, as well as beads, stone tools and much deliberately broken pottery as well as the remains of several sea eagles. Its low entrance passage leads to a rectangular burial chamber which is 3.5 metres high, and has three stalled compartments typical of the Orkney-Cromarty cairns as well as three Maeshowe type side-cells. There were originally low compartments at either end of the main chamber, each with a stone shelf as well, but by the time of the excavation only one remained.

The surviving compartment was full of human bones and beneath its floor a foundation deposit contained bones from another fifteen humans as well as the remains of a white-tailed sea-eagle. There were also large numbers of sea-eagle bones littered throughout the tomb, suggesting that this bird was of particular relevance. They have been radio carbon dated to circa 2450–2050 BC, so were deposited after Beaker People arrived, indicating that here too the new culture continued to bury some of its dead at this old site.

The human remains in this tomb amounted to over 16,000 bones. They were mostly in 'bone piles', although skulls lined the walls, with bigger bones under each one, and the two side-cells at the western end held dozens more skulls, as well as other bones, while the shelved compartment on the south side contained bones but no skulls. Of the eighty-five skulls found sixteen had injuries caused by violent blows to the head, some from blunt instruments like a mace of club, others from spears or arrows and a number from axes or other edged weapons.

Above: Isbister cairn from the east. The excavators found huge quantities of animal and fish bone, including calf and lamb bones from cooked joints of meat, while within the stone enclosure outside the entrance (called a 'hornwork') there were more animal remains. Calves and lambs were slaughtered and cooked here, for consumption or deposition in the enclosure, while lamb cuts were taken into the tomb. By its entrance there were shards from about 46 broken pots, while other pieces were burnt and left in the main chamber.

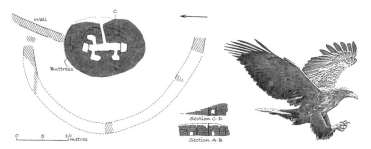

Above: Plan of Isbister. The entrance was arranged so that the sun enters the passageway from the quarter day marking the beginning of summer (the Celtic feast of Beltane) until the quarter day marking summer's end in the mid-August (Lammas). At Beltane, a large stone on the tomb's side wall is lit by a square of sunlight, but after that, as the sun rises higher in the sky towards the midsummer, the square of sunlight gets lower until at the solstice itself the sun only lights up the tomb's floor. Thereafter the sunlight creeps up the back wall again until it is once again a bright square centred on the wall in mid-August.

23

CUWEEN'S CHAMBERED CAIRN

tomb of the dog tribe

Like Isbister, this tomb is thought to date from around 3000 BC. There was no uniformity about building rites and formulae in this period. Cuween is of the so-called Maeshowe type, but is about two hundred years earlier. Cut into solid bedrock and aligned to equinox sunrise, it was an impressive architectural feat. It was first excavated in 1901, when seven human skulls and twenty-four remarkably wolf-like dog skulls were found. The dogs' heads were deposited during the Beaker Culture period; they may have been family totems, like the sea eagles at Isbister and red deer at the Holm of Papa Westray North.

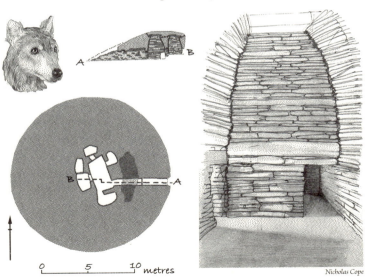

A —————— B

B ———— A

0   5   10 metres

Nicholas Cope

THE HOLM OF PAPA WESTRAY

another Maeshowe-type tomb

At Westray, a tall oblong cairn covers a 20.5m long chamber, accessed by a low entrance-passage, aligned towards the Samhain sun. A series of low doorways, about 40 to 60cms high give access to twelve side-cells, including two double ones. The subdividing walls at each end of the chamber were probably built to strengthen the corbelled roof.

The contents of this tomb were removed long ago, but it has several engraved and pecked designs on particular stones (*see below*), the eyebrow motif recurring on the Westray Venus (*see page 22*). This ambitious tomb is one of three sited at a distant point on this tiny island, looking out over the sea. The earliest known Orkney stone farmhouse was also here, and was inhabited for nine hundred years, so this was a long-established centre of Neolithic culture.

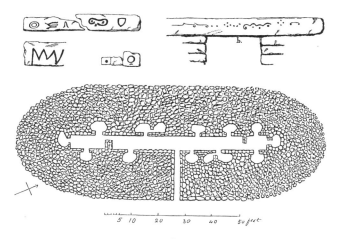

BLACKHAMMER CAIRN, ROUSAY
flints were found

This 13 metre long cairn originally had its external slabs arranged in herringbone patterns. It was built circa 3100–3000 BC but when excavated in 1936 only two bodies were found in it, one in its most westerly compartment, the other in its entrance passage. The other remains included some Unstan ware, a fine flint knife, flint scrapers and bones of sheep, oxen, deer, geese, cormorants and gannets. All of these, including the knife, showed signs of burning. It was formally filled in and sealed before the end of the Neolithic period.

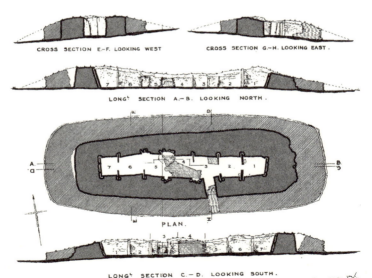

CROSS SECTION E.–F. LOOKING WEST

CROSS SECTION G.–H. LOOKING EAST.

LONG. SECTION A.–B. LOOKING NORTH.

PLAN.

LONG. SECTION C.–D. LOOKING SOUTH.

BLACKHAMMER CAIRN, ROUSAY, ORKNEY.

UNSTAN, ORKNEY MAINLAND

home of Unstan-ware pottery

The Unstan burial chamber has five stalls flanking a 6.4m (21 ft) passageway. Although the original roof is gone, the walls still stand up to almost two metres high (6.6 ft). Pieces of about thirty deliberately broken bowls (*see page 21*) were found. Unstan may predate the major catastrophe of 3200 BC or have been made soon afterwards.

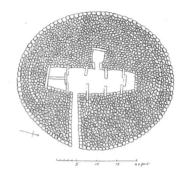

THE TOMB OF QUANTERNESS
Orkney mainland

The interior of Quanterness, another Maeshowe-type tomb, was largely undisturbed when it was examined in the 1970s, and so was only partly excavated and then filled in, to preserve its remaining deposits for the future. It is covered by a large mound, measuring now about 27.5m (90 ft.) in diameter and 3.20m (10ft 6in) in height which originally looked like a truncated cone, 39m(128ft) in circumference at the base and 4.6m (14ft) high.

When this tomb was first opened by George Petrie in 1861, good plans were made of its interior. Six side chambers roofed with corbelling are arranged regularly round its central hall and the floors were covered in dark, earthy clay, containing many human bones along with those of birds and domestic animals. There was also a complete human skeleton in one of the compartments.

The remains of another 157 men, women and children were found during the 1970s excavation. One dated from soon after 3450BC, while the rest were from circa 2850–2790 BC. Only grooved ware pottery was found here, suggesting that its foundation was probably after the circa 3200 BC event but that some earlier remains were brought in from a previous tomb. There had been much mixing of the bones, but the dead seem to have been brought into the tomb as complete bodies, as there were many small bones from hands and feet.

DNA analysis of the bones also revealed that there was "no appreciable consumption of marine protein" by these people; they ate a standard Neolithic diet of sheep and beef and only a little fish.

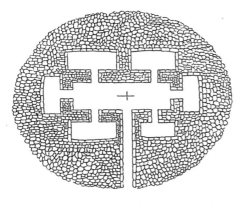

Left: Plan of Quanterness made after George Petrie's excavation in 1861, which appeared in the 1883 book, Scotland in Pagan Times, by Joseph Anderson [1832 - 1916].

Below: Plan of Quanterness made by Prof. Colin Renfrew after his excavation in 1972 - 1973. The passageway is roughly directed towards equinox sunrises. Petrie found an Iron Age round house dug across the entrance to the passageway; several other megalithic tombs were later used as sites for Iron Age houses. This tomb's cairn was about 10m in diameter and formed a 'truncated cone' about 3m high.

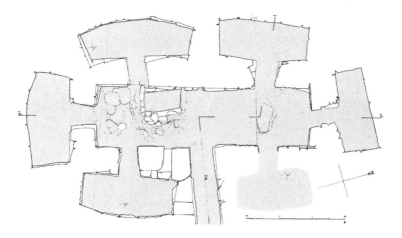

BARNHOUSE
ancient village of Stenness

As well as the great monuments, two particularly significant villages were created after the 3200 BC event. The Barnhouse Settlement is by Harray Loch, only 400m from the Stones of Stenness circle, both dating from c.3100–3000 BC. It consisted of over fifteen small free-standing round houses grouped around an open area used for pottery making, stone knapping, butchery and leather working. The houses had a network of stone drains that led to a common ditch, and all had central hearths, recessed box beds and dressers made from stone slabs. They were mostly rebuilt several times. There was also a very large and well-built double-roomed house with two hearths and six bed recesses which was maintained throughout the life of the village.

Some house sites were demolished c.2600 BC, after which a massive square building with rounded corners and walls about 3m (10 ft) thick was erected on a circular clay platform similar to the one at the recently completed great tomb of Maeshowe, but held in place by a stone revetment wall. As was normal, the building's interior had a central hearth and a dresser, and was about 7m (23 ft) square. This made it a little larger than the tomb of Maeshowe and the Ness of Brodgar's grandest building (Structure 10) to both of which it was carefully interlinked. Barnhouse's entrance was oriented north-west towards Maeshowe's and the midsummer sunset shone down the three metre deep entrance into the great building's interior, just as the midwinter sunset shone into Maeshowe. The entrance causeway to the Stones of Stenness points directly at Barnhouse, while a hearth at the centre of Stenness may have come from a demolished Barnhouse building. Below the floor of the entrance, flanked by two standing stones, lay yet another hearth.

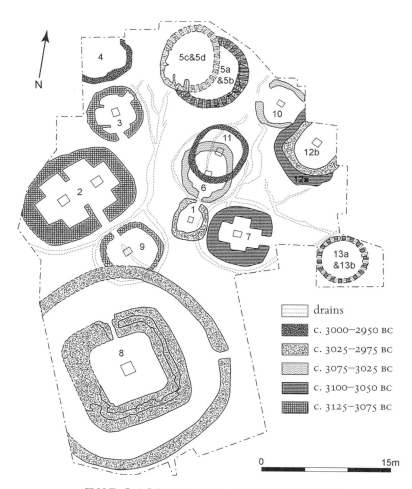

N

4

5c&5d
5a
&5b

3

10

2

11

12b

6

12a

1

9

7

13a
&13b

8

drains

C. 3000—2950 BC

C. 3025—2975 BC

C. 3075—3025 BC

C. 3100—3050 BC

C. 3125—3075 BC

0   15m

THE BARNHOUSE SETTLEMENT

SKARA BRAE

northern Europe's most intact Neolithic village

The impressive Skara Brae settlement is found on the edge of the Bay of
Skaill on the west coast of Orkney's mainland. Occupied from c.3150–
2500 BC, it went through several building phases. The earlier houses were
free standing, but later ones were packed close together, with middens
against their walls and roofed-over passageways, protecting them from
the elements in worsening conditions (*see opposite*).

Skara Brae's roofs would have been supported by beams made from
driftwood or whalebone, while each house had a stone dresser opposite
its low-doored entrance for displaying significant objects and stone-
lined bed recesses and shelves. Elaborate patterns were carved, pecked
or painted onto some stones in the houses and passages, with some
having their decorated surfaces facing inwards, as found elsewhere too.

Skara Brae stone dresser, Hut 1, John Cairns, 1865

Above and below: Skara Brae in its later period, when there were nine closely packed stone houses connected by protective covered passageways (after paintings by Jim Proudfoot for Education Scotland).

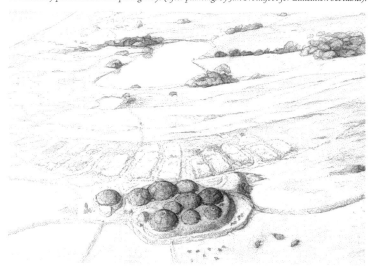

SKARA BRAE DISCOVERIES
hidden hoards and curious carved balls

One building at Skara Brae had shelves built into the interior walls but no beds and was placed slightly apart from the others, surrounded by paving. It seems to have been a workshop, for pieces of chert, a local flint substitute, were found here, as was some Icelandic volcanic pumice, which can wash up on Orkney's beaches and was used for shaping or polishing bone tools and ornaments. Hoards of precious items were also hidden in some of Skara Brae's house walls, and on its floors there was a scatter of bone beads, pins and pendants as well as flint tools, mace heads and some of the curious carved stone balls that are found throughout Scotland (*shown below, and on page 21*). Other materials were used too, including whale and walrus ivory, and some objects were dug in at thresholds as 'closure deposits' when houses were abandoned, a common Neolithic practice. This happened gradually, as erosion by the sea made life increasingly hard, but one house remained inhabited even after it was partly filled with sand.

Skara Brae also yielded three pitchstone flakes from the Isle of Arran, off the Scottish west coast, evidence of long distance contacts, like the local long ivory pins which resemble ones found at Newgrange in Ireland.

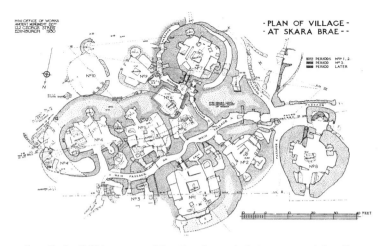

Above: Gordon Childe's 1931 survey of Skara Brae, showing the drainage system with dotted lines.
Below: George Petrie's elevations and drawings of Skara Brae, drawn in 1865.

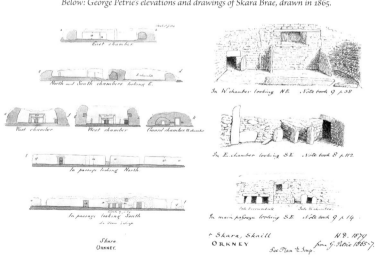

THE NESS OF BRODGAR
a Neolithic ritual site without parallel

The Ness of Brodgar is a narrow isthmus connecting the Ring of Brodgar and the Stones of Stenness. Today it separates the island's two largest inland lochs, although in Neolithic times the freshwater Loch of Stenness lay on one side while a largely boggy area (now the Loch of Harray) was on the other. In 2004, excavations under Nick Card revealed a vast Neolithic ritual complex, which predated the major works at Stonehenge and Avebury complex by hundreds of years. Two giant walls, each more than 100m long and probably 4m high, enclosed a central portion of the Ness, inside which were the remains of over a dozen large buildings and the bones of hundreds of cattle, as well as fine stone artefacts and uniquely decorated stones and ceramics (*see below*).

There had been unusually elaborate buildings here from at least 3500 BC but a new building impetus started after the catastrophe. The buildings are of startling sophistication. Fine stone pathways surround dead straight walls constructed with extraordinary care, which are still two metres high in places, while an enormous drain (a metre wide) ran under the stone pathway to take away rainwater. Small slivers of stones inserted between the main slabs produced perfectly flat walls.

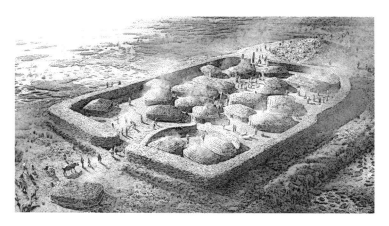

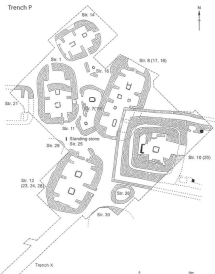

Trench P

Str. 14

Str. 1

Str. 8 (17, 18)

Str. 16

Str. 21

Str. 7(19)

Str. 11

Standing stone

Str. 29   Str. 25

Str. 10 (20)

Str. 12
(23, 24, 28)

Str. 26

Str. 30

Trench X

0   10m

Above: Artist's impression of the Neolithic complex on the Ness of Brodgar. These buildings must have been profoundly important for Neolithic Orcadians. The rituals performed here are unknown, but astronomical sightings were clearly made, and the rites performed will have involved the dead as well as the living as a few human bones were deposited in special places. The many hearths in the Ness's buildings were probably for preparing food for great feasts and many broken stone mace heads have been found too—as at many other Neolithic sites, these seem to be from rituals performed for the departed, perhaps with one half of each mace left with the dead and the other retained by the living.

Left: Plan of excavations at the Ness by Nick Card, showing building 10.

THE NESS'S GREATEST BUILDING
and its precursor

The enclosing Ness site wall became ever more massive as building works continued, until the site's greatest building, Structure 10, was started (*see opposite*). Several buildings were demolished to make way for this and it was finished around 2,900 BC, and refitted 100 years later.

Although Structure 10 was by far the most impressive feature on the Ness site in its day, it was not the first on this scale. An earlier large building, now called Structure 27, stood at the southern tip of the Ness of Brodgar peninsula. It was a little smaller, 12m wide by over 17m long, but it was outstandingly well built, with thick rubble walls, whose well-finished external facing had pick-dressing on many stones. There was also a paved area around it with stone drains underneath it, suggesting that many people came here. The building's interior wall surfaces were elaborately arranged with 4m long *orthostats*, stones much greater in length than depth, lying along the wall bases with upright slabs between them, in the manner of the stalled cairns, (although this was not a tomb). Like the ones at Structure 10 and Maeshowe, these orthostats may have come from an earlier structure, perhaps even a stone circle, and were so carefully laid that their levels differed by little more than two centimetres. Above them long upright slabs covered the internal walls like planks and like the buildings on the Ness site it was roofed with stone slates. At some time in the late Neolithic, Structure 27 was taken down and its foundations buried under a 4m high midden mound, over 70m in diameter. This seems mainly to consist of residue from many great feasts. The formal burial of old ritual structures under great mounds happened at many sites in the British Isles, and the resultant mounds were greatly respected.

Above: Structure 10, around 3000 BC, by Kenny Arne Lang Antonsen and Jimmy John Antonsen, shown with a massive stone roof with eaves extending over the paved walkway around the building. Its entrance was flanked by two standing stones, and led to the inner chamber. This was originally a square room with rounded internal corners, embellished with pick and pecked decorated stones and several different coloured sandstones. After the redesign the room was given a cruciform shape.

Above: Map of the sites around the Ness. A melting pot of communities seems to have come here during the main construction period, with numerous contacts with Ireland and southern Britain. The genetic origins of the Orkney vole also indicate that people must have come here from the Belgian region around 3000 BC, while the Orcadians' amber beads were from the Baltic.

MAESHOWE
Orkney Mainland

The great tomb of Maeshowe dates from circa 2800 BC, and so was built during the last major phase of building activity at the Ness. It is was probably built on the site of an earlier structure, possibly a stone circle, as it stands on a circular henge-like platform with its midwinter sunset-aligned entrance pointing at that of the Ness of Brodgar, while the slightly later great building at Barness was also aligned towards it.

The entrance was carefully set up so that the setting sun would light up the back wall of the chamber for twenty days on either side of the winter solstice with the setting of Venus, the Evening Star, also being observed once every eight years. This arrangement must have held great meaning for Maeshowe's creators. A large stone in the entrance passage is designed to be moved across it to reduce the beam of light entering the chamber, much like the lightbox at Newgrange, constructed c.3100 BC. The highly decorated passage grave at Gavrinis in Brittany, dated to c.3500 BC also has alignments to the winter solstice sun as well as to the rising moon at its southernmost extreme setting.

Left and below: Illustrations from the 1861 excavation of Maes Howe, from the 1862 Proceedings of the Society of Antiquaries in Scotland.

At 2.35pm on the winter solstice, the sun shines on the back of the chamber for 17 minutes, before disappearing behind Ward Hill and then reappearing 17 minutes later, only to finally set at 3.20pm.

On every eighth year at 5.00pm, Venus does the same, being visible from the chamber, before setting at 5.15pm. behind Ward Hill. Fifteen minutes later, Venus reappears on the other side of Ward Hill, and is seen for two more minutes, before setting for a second time.

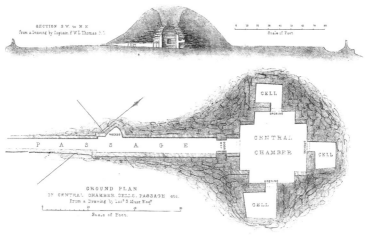

SECTION S.W. to N.E.
from a Drawing by Captain F.W.L. Thomas R.N.

Scale of Feet

GROUND PLAN
OF CENTRAL CHAMBER CELLS, PASSAGE etc.
From a Drawing by Ino.S Mair Esq.

Scale of Feet.

P A S S A G E

CELL

OPENING

CENTRAL

CHAMBER

CELL

OPENING

CELL

THE RING OF BRODGAR
a perfect circle

Some major changes happened on Orkney around the start of the Beaker period. The Ring of Brodgar henge and stone circle were built soon after 2500 BC, a kilometre to the north of the Ness. Unlike Stenness, this is a Class 2 henge, with two entrances directly opposite each other, probably indicating some difference in ritual usage.

Brodgar is the third largest henge in the British Isles, measuring 104m (341 ft) in diameter. Originally it had about 60 stones, not quite as huge as those at Stenness, of which 27 remain, the tallest on the south and west sections of the ring. Its enclosing ditch, which was carved into the bedrock in sections, is up to 3m (9.8 ft) deep, 9m (30 ft) wide and 380m (1,250 ft) in circumference. As with the Stones of Stenness, Brodgar's stones came from different parts of Orkney. It is easy to envisage people arriving from various localities with their own stones, each one honouring a community, its ancestors and its territory, and then erecting them and digging sections of the ditch.

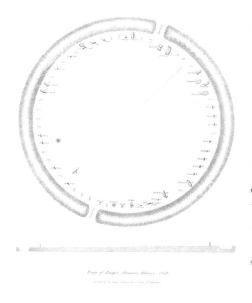

Left: Earliest accurate plan of the Ring of Brodgar, made in 1852 by Lt Thomas of HM Survey Vessel Woodlark. Excavating the ditch may have taken about 80,000 hours and the workforces must have been expertly directed, as the Ring had to be first set up so that a person standing at its centre can see the midwinter sun setting behind the Hill of Hoy, or the minor southern setting of the moon at the cliffs of Hellia on Hoy, while the minor southern moonrise occurs at a notch on Mid Hill, to the south-east. The winter and summer solstice sunrises and sunsets also align with particular stones and notches in hills on the horizon, and the setting equinox sun can be viewed from the Comet Stone, glancing off Brodgar's westernmost stone.

Ring of Brogar Stennes, Orkney. 1849.

Facing page: View of the Ring of Brodgar from Rev. Barry's History of the Orkney Islands, 1805. Below: Early engraving based on the 1775 painting by John Frederick Miller (see title page). Long use of the site is shown in many broken Beaker and Bronze Age stone mace-heads and flint arrowheads

CHANGING RITES AT STENNESS

from moon to midwinter feasting

At the Stenness ring, significant changes also happened during the Beaker Period and the Bronze Age. At the centre of the circle a large stone lined hearth was inserted, similar to those found in Neolithic houses, with four large stone slabs dug in upright to edge it. Traces of cremated animal bone, charcoal and broken pottery in the hearth suggest that feasting happened here. This is not surprising, research at Stonehenge has showed that many people came to the Stonehenge area from far and wide, including from Orkney, for great ceremonies, bringing pigs and cattle to be slaughtered and cooked for midwinter feasts, so it seems likely that similar events may have happened on Orkney too. Professor Colin Richards, who excavated the Barnhouse Settlement near Stenness, has suggested that the hearth may have come from there, and a recent excavation has revealed that a massive wooden beam or tree trunk, previously stood where the hearth now is. Then, at about the same time as the hearth was dug in, a rough stone path was laid from it towards the entrance and stopped beside two sockets for standing stones.

These stones seem to have formed a monumental entrance to a two-metre square timber structure, and some wood from it has given a radio-carbon date of circa 2150 BC. The eastern and western sides of this timber structure lined up with the two stones, which were presumably removed when the timber building was dismantled. Moreover, close to the hearth two angular slabs stand side by side, with a large prone stone beside them. These too were part of the layout created between the hearth and the timber structure, during the Beaker or Bronze Age redevelopment of the site.

Above: The Stones of Stenness by Muirhead Bone [1876-1953]. In the 1960s Professor Alexander Thom suggested that Stenness had been set up to observe the moon's extreme northern and southern risings and settings, including the extraordinary phenomenon of the major lunar standstill. Recent investigations by Gail Higginbottom and Roger Clay have proved that this was the case.

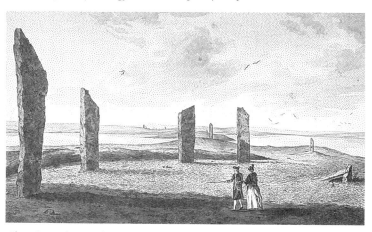

Above: Stones of Stenness by John Cleveley, 1772. Calanais, on the Isle of Lewis, the only other major stone circle from which the moon could be seen moving very close to the southern horizon during the lunar standstill, seems to have been created at much the same time as Stenness.

THE END OF THE OLD ORDER
death and disaster

The copper and gold-working Beaker people probably came from the area around the Rhine delta to the British Isles circa 2450 BC. Orkney had been affected by rising sea levels that caused the Atlantic to break into the freshwater Loch of Stenness circa 2500 BC, drowning land around the Ness of Brodgar, and possibly a henge beside the Bay of Firth. An ash or dust cloud from a possible volcano eruption or asteroid strike also seems to have stunted growth around this time, bringing severe hardship. Between 2354 and 2345 BC, Irish and British tree rings show a similar pattern to the 3200 BC episode. Within five years the Neolithic population would have consumed their final harvest, their domestic animals and the seed corn. Few can have survived. The metal-workers may have arrived into a largely deserted island in the 2340s.

DNA analysis shows that a major population upheaval occurred. Within two centuries 90% of the genes of the population of the British Isles were those of lighter-skinned, often fair-haired and light-eyed Beaker people from central Europe. An early form of yersinia pestis disease (precursor to the bubonic plague) also appeared around this time, spreading person to person, with victims identified across north-western Europe. Few descendants of the original olive-skinned and dark-eyed Neolithic people are found in the subsequent population.

Skara Brae spiked object

Skara Brae lintel

Newgrange

House 7, Skara Brae

Brodgar Stones, Stenness

King of Bledlow exhibition proof *[signature]* 1996

Hackwell Point exhibition proof *[signature]* 1996

DISTURBANCES ON ORKNEY

here comes the metal

Part of the old population clearly did survive, as both the DNA evidence and the continued use of old ritual sites reveal. It was a time of great change, however, and circa 2450 to 2350 BC, a great ceremonial feast was staged. Ness's greatest building, Structure 10, was taken down and buried under thousands of tons of rubble and midden built up in layers to make a large mound, after which a final feast (or several) was held. Four hundred head of cattle were slaughtered, roasted and eaten, and the bones split open to get at the marrows, after which the carcasses of red deer were placed over the cattle bones. This event mirrored the feastings at Structure 27, which had also helped create a vast mound. Doubtless these mounds were of great significance to the people, but the only clues we have about who attended the last banquet on the mound over Structure 10 are two small Beaker Culture objects found above the feasting residues: a pottery shard and an arrowhead.

The pottery shard is particularly interesting for it closely resembles Beaker ware from Durrington Walls, close to Stonehenge (*see caption, opposite top*). And excavations at Durrington have provided further connections to the Ness. Remains of feasts from the mid-third millennium BC were found and these too seem to have happened at midwinter. Presumably this was also when the last feasts at the Ness happened, for this way of cutting back on surplus livestock had been practiced since early Neolithic times (*lower, opposite*). Most intriguingly of all, DNA analysis of bones from animals slaughtered for these midwinter Stonehenge feasts reveals that many of the animals had come all the way from Northeast Scotland!

Left: Beaker ware, typical of the Durrington type. Structure 10's pottery shard resembles Beaker ware from Durrington Walls, close to Stonehenge, showing the strength of the connections between their Beaker communities. Durrington is an important site, with two ritual rings and a large number of houses in it, which were probably only used during gatherings for ritual activities and feasting. The Ness shard, however, was made on Orkney. A second pottery fragment also found at the Ness is equally remarkable as it is from a tiny perforated 'incense cup' and only four others of this type are known. These are all from the Stonehenge area and associated with Beaker Period burials; they were possibly used for carrying embers or incense to or from a funeral pyre.

Above: Beaker people feasting (after Luis Pascual). Five-day-long 'New Year Feastings' were still being held on Orkney in the eighteenth century. Until recently many north European farmers solved fodder shortages by slaughtering surplus livestock at mid-winter and laying on a great feast. The new beer would be drunk as well.

THE CRANTIT TOMB
Kirkwall, Orkney mainland

An extraordinary amalgamation of Neolithic and Beaker customs came to light in 1998 when an underground tomb was found at Crantit, near Kirkwall. It is a miniature stalled chamber tomb of circa 2130 BC, almost round in plan with three 'stalls' divided by upright slabs around an open central area and a corbelled roof. It was created entirely below ground level, as was normal Beaker burial custom (whereas Neolithic chamber tombs were constructed on the surface and covered by cairns). Moreover, the interior is only one metre high, while the main chambers of the old tombs were tall enough to stand in. This tomb must be akin to the custom of placing Beaker-style burials in old chambered cairns, perhaps because surviving groups of the old Neolithic population tried to maintain some old customs in the new era.

Crantit was dug into an Ice Age moraine, a low hill of glacially rounded rocks, into which two Bronze Age cists were also dug. The excavators found a polished stone ball, some textile and pottery fragments and the disarticulated bones of a woman over thirty, a teenage girl and a child of about four to six in one stall, as well as some skull fragments of a fourth person in another cell.

There were also interesting designs carved on one of the stones supporting Crantit's roof and a 'lightbox', an opening in the roof slabs that let sunlight into the tomb at the cross-quarter days around November 5th (Guy Fawkes night in fact replaced a much older fire festival) and February 6th. The 'lightbox' and the entrance were closed with clay and stones soon after the burials. It and the movable stone at Maeshowe are later versions of the 'lightboxes' at Newgrange and Carrowkeel in Ireland.

Above: The Crantit tomb. The tomb was under an unremarkable hillock in a field and lay undisturbed until a tractor dislodged one of its roof slabs and revealed the tomb beneath.

Left: At Crantit, the human bones were jumbled together in one of the stalls along with some pottery shards. It was a remarkable echo of Neolithic practices, while on the slopes around it there were several more normal Bronze Age cist burials, which would also have had little mounds over them. At one of the earliest Neolithic sites, the Links of Noltland on Westray (where three early carvings of human figures were found, including the Westray Venus, see page 20), there is evidence for a foundation ritual: the inverted skulls of ten cattle were built into the base of a wall, with their horns stuck into the ground. Interestingly, the first Neolithic villages in the Near East had skull shrines, as did later ones in Anatolia.

THE BRONZE AGE & BEYOND
and four gold disks

A further period of bad climatic conditions, circa 2200-2000 BC, made life very hard here, but even so the bronze-making culture reached Orkney soon after the rest of the Britain circa 2100 BC. Few bronze objects have been found, but there are Bronze Age period remains from across the archipelago. These include the ruins of a farmstead and a burnt mound on Auskerry, two houses on Holm of Faray and a settlement mound at Tofts Ness on Sanday. The best known on the mainland are a ceremonial sweat lodge near Isbister cairn and the many burial mounds into which the remains of the dead were placed in small cists or urns, including the sixteen mounds at the Knowes of Trotty and the Plumcake Mound near the Ring of Brodgar. Each one covered the tomb of an individual or sometimes a couple, indicating a society where the significance of particular persons rather than the ancestors was revered.

In 1858, four gold disks were found in a cist inside the largest of the Knowes of Trotty mounds along with 27 amber beads, some pendants and a few burnt bones. The design of the disks is similar to ones from the south of England and the gold is Scottish, while the amber is from the Baltic. It was probably the grave of a high status woman.

Left: Artist's impression of a woman wearing the four c.2000 BC gold disks found in the largest of the Knowes of Trotty mounds. Until recent times, the Orcadians believed that such mounds were homes of ancestors, giants or otherworld beings called Trows. It was taboo to damage the mounds and tales abound of their magical powers, as spirit feasting halls or places where people could cross from one world into the other. One story tells how a fiddler one midsummer night, when the music-loving Hill Trows come out of their mounds, saw a stone door open in a green mound, so he entered and found a world where everyone was young and danced to his tunes. He returned after what seemed only a day to find that centuries had passed by.

Left: The Salt Knowe: Orkney's Silbury Hill. Along with the Ring of Brodgar the Salt Knowe seems to belong to the last phase of creating the Ness ritual landscape. This huge mound dominates the countryside south-west of the Ring beside Stenness loch and its diameter of 40 metres (131 feet) by 33 metres (108 feet) and height of six metres (19.6 feet), are very similar to those of Maeshowe. When the Orkney College Geophysics Unit scanned it with ground-penetrating radar in 2008, they found it to be a massive man-made mound of earth, with no internal structure, confirming the report of the antiquarian James Farrer who excavated Maeshowe and the Salt Knowe in 1861.

VIKING VISITORS
and rowdy runes

Maeshowe was closed along with many other ancient ritual centres during the Beaker Period, and a very different world developed here during the Iron Age, but Maeshowe was visited and reopened by the Vikings. They rebuilt its surrounding wall in the 9th century and told in one of their epic poems, the *Orkneyinga Saga*, how a chief, Harald Maddadarson, broke into it in the 12th century through its roof, while Earl Rognvald of Orkney was away on a crusade to Jerusalem.

Over 30 runic inscriptions cover its chamber's walls, the largest number in any one place. Most simply identify the inscriber: "*Haermund Hardaxe carved these runes*" although some tell a little more: "*Ingigerth is the most beautiful of women*" one reads, while a less polite one says "*Þorný fucked, Helgi carved*". Another tantalisingly proclaims "*To the north-west is a great hidden treasure. It was hidden long ago*", although another says "*It is surely true what I say, that treasure was carried off in three nights before the men from Jerusalem broke into this howe*". These would have been Earl Rognvald's warriors returning from their crusade. (*See too captions opposite.*)

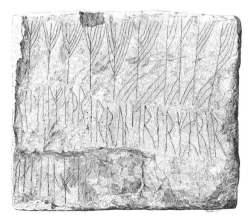

Above: Vikings arriving in Orkney in the late 8th century.

Left: Viking graffiti on Maeshowe Stone No.20 proudly says "These runes were carved by the man most skilled in runes in the western ocean." Another stone in the chamber then adds "With the axe of Gauk Trandilsson of the South land."

Facing page: Viking graffiti on Maeshowe Stone No.9 says "Ingibjorg, the fair widow. Many a women has gone stooping in here. A great show. Erlingr."

CONTINUING THEMES
dancing and marriage in the stones

Not only did so much of Orkney's finest prehistoric structures and some of its customs survive the ravages of time, but legends abound too, of the amazing achievements of the vanished Neolithic people:

One dark and starry night, a long time ago, a group of fearsome giants crossed the causeway on to the Ness of Brodgar. They gathered in a field with Stenness Loch to its left and Harray Loch to the right and decided to dance. From the folds of his cloak the fiddler took out an ancient fiddle and began a swirling reel. Upon hearing the music, his companions joined hands and, whooping and shouting like fools, formed a circle and danced. The ground trembled beneath their feet as they whirled round and round, faster and faster. So great was their enjoyment that they forgot to keep an eye on the eastern horizon and lost all thought as to how quickly the night was passing. Then, before they knew it, the morning sun crept into the sky behind them and with a shriek and a moan the newborn rays of light touched the dancing giants. No sooner had the golden light touched their skin than they turned into cold, hard stone. And there they remain to this day.

The petrified giants of Stenness still stand, and so does their fiddler—the nearby Comet Stone. Other important monoliths include the Watch Stone, a massive stone (5.6m high) towering over the Brig o' Brodgar, which was originally one of a pair making a portal on the approach to the Ness of Brodgar, (the stump of the other one was removed during road widening in 1930). The Barnhouse Stone to its south-east was positioned between Maeshowe and the Stenness Stones so that the setting winter solstice sun is seen directly above the Barnhouse Stone from Maeshowe, as its last rays penetrate into the tomb. The Odin Stone (*opposite*) stood 140m to the north of the Stones of Stenness until its toppling by a 'ferrylouper', Captain W. Mackay, in 1814.

Above: The Odin Stone, drawn in 1805 by Elizabeth, Marchioness of Stafford, was destroyed in the 19th century. It had a hole through it and had probably been part of the ritual landscape from the earliest times. A Viking period tale speaks of a man who, when the moon was nearing its standstill, 'for nine moons at midnight, when the moon was full, he went nine times on his bare knees around the Odin Stone of Stainness' and then looked through its hole hoping for a vision of the future.

Above: Other rites were also observed at the Odin Stone: babies had their heads put into the stone's hole to stop them getting palsy and until the 19th century marriage ceremonies were performed here during the five days of the New Year Feasting; young lovers would first visit the Stenness Stones to make their promises after which they went to the Odin Stone where they held hands through the hole (see below) and prayed to keep their oaths of fidelity to each other. After this the young pair would walk around the Brodgar Ring and often 'proceed to Consummation without further Ceremony'.

EPILOGUE

the building continues

The Orcadians continued to create great monuments after the Bronze Age. Imposing stone-walled roundhouses appeared from about 700 BC, and then a little later much larger Iron Age round stone-walled forts called brochs were built. These were probably inspired by the roundhouses as forts for local chiefs and became popular status symbols, for there are 50 brochs on Orkney, and nearly seven hundred more across Northern and Western Scotland and the Western Isles. It may be that Orkney had once again invented a monument type that was copied across a wide area.

After Sigurd the Stout, the Viking jarl of Orkney and the Northern Isles, became a Christian in 995, some Norwegian and German clerics built churches here in their preferred style, with round towers at the west end. Only St Magnus on Egilsay survives, but when Magnus's nephew, Rognvald Kali Kolsson, claimed the Earldom of Orkney, he had a "stone minster" built in his uncle's memory. It was begun in 1137, probably by English masons who had worked on Durham Cathedral, and so Kirkwall's own superb Romanesque cathedral arose, a worthy counterpart to Orkney's Neolithic monuments.